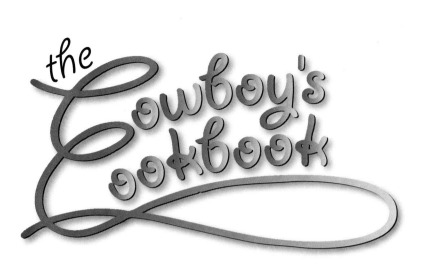

the Cowboy's Cookbook

MORE THAN 50 TRAILBLAZING RECIPES FROM THE AMERICAN WEST

COURAGE BOOKS
AN IMPRINT OF RUNNING PRESS
PHILADELPHIA • LONDON

CLB 4962
This edition first published in 1998 in the United States by Courage Books.
© CLB International
A division of Quadrillion Publishing Ltd, Godalming, Surrey, Gu7 1XW, England

Printed and bound in Singapore by Tien Wah Press.

9 8 7 6 5 4 3 2 1
Digit on the right indicates the number of this printing

Library of Congress Cataloging-in-Publication Number 97-66744

ISBN 0-7624-0275-X

This book was designed and produced by CLB International
Godalming, Surrey, England, GU7 1XW

Contributor (pages 6–9) **and consultant:** Cathy Luchetti

Project management: Jo Richardson

Design: Liz Chidlow

Illustration: Philip Chidlow

Food photography: Amanda Heywood

Home economy: Elizabeth Wolf-Cohen

Antique photography: Neil Sutherland

(see page 80 for full acknowledgments)

Production: Ruth Arthur and Neil Randles

Color reproduction: HBM Print Ltd

Published by Courage Books, an imprint of
Running Press Book Publishers
125 South Twenty-second Street
Philadelphia, Pennsylvania 19103-4399

Contents

❧ CHUCK WAGON COOKING ❧

Cowboy cooking reached its peak during the great trail drives, when wranglers, longhorns, and the chuck wagon cooks kicked up clouds of dust on their way west. Though the dust has long since settled, the hearty foods of the open range live on, linking past to present in a style both delicious and authentic.

"Chow" was served up three times a day to cowboys who "rode the line" to mend fences or who rounded up wayward strays. Ingredients were scarce and trail conditions primitive, but nothing could keep the chuck wagon cook—whose job was the most demanding on the trail—from whipping up hearty trail fare using cast-iron Dutch ovens and heavy, cast-iron

skillets. Such cooking, simply served around the campfire under the big sky, has led to a tradition of hearty, fresh-cooked meals that continues on ranches today.

The first cowboy menus of the early 1800s were as sparse and lonely as the landscape itself, usually consisting of jerked beef, biscuits, whiskey, and coffee stored in the wrangler's saddlebags. Since pots, pans, or skillets were too heavy to carry, the solitary trail hands sent out to round up strays heated their rations over a crackling fire, using sticks to spear and turn the food. Range riding was an endless blend of hard work, boredom, and bland food, often followed by hunger when their meager stocks were depleted.

The tradition of cowboy cooking reached a new level in 1866, when

rancher Charles Goodnight designed the first chuck wagon. By then, large cattle ranchers employed teams of cowboys to ride east in the great trail drives, each a vast, sprawling migration of steers, strays, horses, and, most important, the chuck wagon. Goodnight's simple, ox-drawn prototype was merely a wooden cupboard fixed to the back of an army wagon, but it revolutionized cooking on the trail. The chuck box tucked neatly into the tail of a wagon or popped out to serve as a work table, providing storage space for cast-iron skillets, lidded pots, hooks, ovens, and irons, as well as 30 days' worth of supplies, including dried beans, preserved meats, biscuit fixin's, molasses, dried fruits, and the cowboy's favorite dessert, canned tomatoes. Individual compartments stored sugar, salt, pepper, and condiments, while a locked cupboard allowed the trail boss to secure important documents and medicine. Fresh meat was either wrapped in a bedroll and swung from a nearby tree for tenderizing, or stored in burlap for cleanliness.

But most important, the new-style chuck wagons were "cook-sized," or at least 4 feet high, waterproofed, and fitted with a sleeping bunk for the cook's convenience. For the first time, the cook rated a comfy, indoor sleeping space, leading to improved temperament as well as better meals. An unhappy "Cookie" meant unhappy trail hands, and everyone on the round-up suffered.

Over the period from 1870 to 1883, an estimated 40 million head of buffalo were killed on the Great Plains, opening up the vast grasslands for ranchers to winter-graze cattle on the favored bluegrass before shipping them East. Cowboys lost no time in making the most of any stray survivors, cooking up thick steaks of the naturally lean and tasty meat (page 27). Other meat treats along the trail, bringing a more than welcome change from the regular beef-and-beans fare, were provided by shooting wild game for the cooking pot—venison (page 32), antelope, a variety of game birds (page 20), rabbit (page 30), and squirrel.

Without refrigerators, cowboy cooks often relied on salt pork, rather than fresh pork, to add flavor to their endless pots of beans. Or, they would use beef drippings to quickly fry leftover pieces of beef before adding the beans.

Literally every part of an animal was used, if it could be, to provide food for hungry cowhands. "Son-of-a-Bitch Stew" (page 18)—more delicately called "Son-of-a-Gun Stew" on the odd occasion when a woman was present—was made from a cow's innards, being taken directly from the slaughtered carcass to a huge Dutch oven. The most important ingredient, credited with adding a rich succulence to the stew, was the marrow gut—one of the stomach chambers of an unweaned calf. Frugal chuck wagon cooks, who never wasted a scrap of beef, apparently made up large pots of "Son-of-a Bitch Stew" each time a cow was slaughtered, and refused to empty the cooking pot until all was eaten.

☙ CAMPFIRE COOKING ☙

The trail cook's first task upon arriving at a new camp was to dig a trench for the fire, stacking the logs so the fire would draw freely and quickly create sizzling coals. Then, he erected a pot rack of two iron poles with a long crossbar in between. From this hung pots of slowly simmering stew, or the inevitable pot of beans.

But the most important piece of equipment carried in the chuck wagon was the cast-iron Dutch oven. These versatile pots came in a range of sizes, up to 16 inches across, with three or four small legs on the bottom for sitting on top of red-hot coals. Coals were also heaped over the lid, creating such heat that an iron rod, or gonch hook, was needed to uncover the sizzling oven.

No reasonable cook went on a trail drive with less than four Dutch ovens, for cooking all kinds of dishes.

No reasonable cook went on a trail drive with less than four Dutch ovens, since they were needed for frying, boiling, and simmering as well as for whipping up dozens of baking powder biscuits. Six men could go through 66 biscuits in a sitting, and very often, a trail crew could be close to 30. The Dutch oven solved the problem of how to bake without a stove, while baking powder solved the problem of how to bake without yeast. Fruit cobblers (page 34), made with the wild berries gathered along the trail, were a popular cowboy dessert and provided a toothsome relief from the more usual puddings made from the ever-present beef suet. Similar to a single-crust deep-dish pie but with a baking-powder biscuit topping, cobblers were so named because the toppings are rough and bumpy, like a cobbled street. Again, they were baked in a Dutch oven. Another more everyday, eggless dessert was a concoction of rice and molasses, which was cooked long and slow in the Dutch oven until nearly carmelized.

In fact, cowboy cooking was a series of innovations. Yeast was not available until 1868, and cooks on the trail had to make sourdough bread and biscuits from a "starter" made from sun-fermented potatoes and potato cooking water (pages 66–69). Sourdough bread and biscuits, or "pinch-offs" as they were originally known (page 68), were again baked in the ingenious Dutch oven over hot coals, with extra coals placed on top of the pot's thick, concave lid.

Beans, a cowboy staple along with the sourdough biscuits, beef, and coffee, were often cooked in a tightly sealed can buried in a hole in the ground with hot coals (page 22), so that they could be left unattended. Some cowboy historians write it was a matter of honor for anyone riding past a "bean hole," as it was called, to stop and make sure the coals were still burning. When beans were on the breakfast menu, cooks would leave a pan of beans buried overnight, and the hands coming in from their two-hour shifts on watch would make sure the coals were still glowing.

Coffee usually came as raw green beans to be roasted in a skillet over the open fire. Chicken-fried steak (page 12), a firm trail favorite, demanded softening up with a mallet in order to please the cowboy palate.

Rise and shine

Every predrawn morning brought hungry men stumbling through the dark, ready for mugs of ink-black coffee and hearty grub that could stick to their ribs. The cowboy's day started before sunrise, and by the time the dishes were washed and the wagon packed, it might be as late as 5 a.m. Strong black coffee started the day—one chuck wagon recipe instructs: "Take a pound of coffee, add water, boil for half an hour. Throw in horseshoe; if it sinks, add more coffee." Water for the coffee was often drawn from the cattle's supply—a stretch of dammed off stream—even when, from time to time, the odd dead cow was found in its murky depths. No wonder the strength of the coffee was such an issue with the cowpunchers!
Cathy Luchetti

On the Trail

CHICKEN-FRIED STEAK WITH TEXAS SAUCE

Makes 4 servings

"Texas sauce" was the gravy made with fat in a skillet after a steak was fried. This recipe uses milk, but cooks would have used whatever water was available—even if it came from streams where the cattle drank. Ramon F. Adams recalls in Come an' Get It, The Story of the Old Cowboy Cook, *that "No cowboy worthy of the calling wanted his steaks any way but fried." [1]*

¼ cup all-purpose flour

½ teaspoon garlic salt

Pinch of cayenne pepper, or to taste

Freshly ground black pepper, to taste

4 steaks, such as sirloin, 6–8 ounces each and ½-inch thick

About 2 tablespoons vegetable oil or beef drippings

1 cup milk

1. Combine the flour, garlic salt, cayenne pepper, and black pepper in a plastic bag and shake. Add the steaks, one at a time, shaking until lightly coated. Remove the steak from the bag and shake any excess flour back into the bag.

2. Heat the oil or melt the drippings in a large skillet over medium-high heat. Add the steaks to the pan and fry for 3 minutes on each side for rare, or 5 minutes on each side for well-done. Fry the steaks in batches if there is not enough room in the pan, keeping each fried steak warm in a low oven until they are all fried. Add extra oil or drippings to the pan as necessary.

3. Meanwhile, to make the Texas sauce, empty the flour mixture remaining in the bag into a small bowl, and stir in 2 tablespoons of the milk to make a smooth paste.

4. When all the steaks have been fried, pour the milk paste into the pan, stirring to scrape up any crisp bits on the bottom. Lower the heat to medium and add the remaining milk, stirring continuously until the gravy thickens and bubbles.

5. Adjust the seasoning, if necessary. Serve the steaks with the Texas sauce, and pan-fried potatoes or Sourdough Pinch-Offs (page 68).

CHILI CON CARNE

Makes 4–6 servings

Meat spoilage was a constant problem for chuck wagon cooks, and this hot-and-spicy beef stew was first developed as a way to disguise the unpleasant flavor of meat about to become rancid. The original trail chili consisted of just coarsely ground beef and tiny red chiles. Eventually, beans and other vegetables were included in the dish. Chili has the best flavor if made a day in advance and reheated.

2 tablespoons vegetable oil

1 large onion, chopped

1 red bell pepper, cored, seeded, and diced

1 green bell pepper, cored, seeded, and diced

1 fresh red chile, seeded and very finely chopped, or to taste

2 teaspoons cayenne pepper, or to taste

1 teaspoon ground cumin

1 teaspoon garlic salt

1 teaspoon dried oregano

Salt and freshly ground black pepper, to taste

2 pounds lean ground beef

2 (16-ounce) cans chopped tomatoes

1 (16-ounce) can red kidney beans, drained and rinsed

1 (8-ounce) can corn kernels, drained

1. Heat the oil in a large, deep skillet or flameproof casserole over medium heat. Add the onion, bell peppers, and fresh chile and fry, stirring, for 5–7 minutes, until softened.

2. Stir in the cayenne pepper, cumin, garlic salt, oregano, and salt and pepper. Continue frying for 2 minutes, stirring occasionally.

3. Add the beef, using the back of the spoon to break it up, and stir until it browns lightly. Pour off any excess fat.

4. Stir in the tomatoes with the juice and the beans. Bring to a boil. Lower the heat, cover, and simmer for 15 minutes.

5. Stir in the corn. Re-cover and continue to simmer for 5 minutes longer, until all the flavors blend. If the chili is too liquid, however, leave uncovered and lightly boil until the liquid reduces. Adjust the seasoning if necessary.

The loud "ding" of the iron triangle announced meals three times a day. Each cook had his characteristic rhythm, the intensity of the call often reflecting the chef's temperament!

14

TEXAS LONGHORN CHILI

Makes 4–6 servings

Contrary to a common misconception, a bowl of chili should taste of more than just "heat." This recipe uses fresh Anaheim, or common green, chiles for a mild flavor and commercial cayenne pepper for heat.

Vegetable oil or beef drippings

2 pounds boneless beef chuck, trimmed and cut into 2-inch cubes

3 large onions, finely chopped

4 large cloves garlic, crushed

2 fresh Anaheim chiles, seeded and finely sliced (see Cook's Tip), or to taste

1 tablespoon cayenne pepper, or to taste

1 tablespoon sugar

2 teaspoons fresh thyme leaves, or 1 teaspoon dried

1 teaspoon dried oregano leaves

1 (16-ounce) can chopped tomatoes

1 cup beef stock or water

Salt and freshly ground black pepper, to taste

Finely chopped green onions (scallions), to garnish

Hot boiled rice, to serve

1. Heat 2 tablespoons of oil or drippings in a large flameproof casserole over medium-high heat. Add the beef cubes, in batches, and fry until browned. Remove each batch with a draining spoon and add extra oil or drippings if necessary.

2. Stir in the onions and garlic. Cover them with a sheet of crumpled, wet waxed paper, cover the pan, and sweat the ingredients for 20 minutes, until softened and starting to brown. Return all the beef to the pan.

3. Stir in the chiles, cayenne pepper, sugar, thyme and oregano, tomatoes with the juice, beef stock, and salt and pepper. Bring to a boil, then lower the heat, cover, and simmer for 1 hour.

4. Partially uncover the pan and continue simmering the chili for 30 minutes longer, or until the meat is very tender and most of the liquid has evaporated.

5. Adjust the seasoning if necessary. Serve hot with green onions (scallions) sprinkled over the top and accompanied with freshly boiled rice.

COOK'S TIP

Anaheim chiles are sold in supermarkets. If not available, use a fresh poblano chile or its dried version, the ancho chile For a hotter chili, use fresh jalapeño or serrano chiles. Or, use dried cayenne, pasilla, or pequin chiles.

Red-Hot BBQ Beef Ribs

Makes 4 servings

On an average day, a trail cook had to prepare three meals before packing up his chuck wagon and moving on to the next day's camp. This meant there wasn't time for barbecuing, which requires regular attention. Cow hands could only hope for succulent, spicy ribs like these when the wagon stayed put for several days.

4 meaty beef ribs, 10–12 inches long and weighing about 1 pound each

Vegetable oil for grilling or broiling

SIZZLING BARBECUE SAUCE

2 tablespoons vegetable oil or beef drippings

1 large onion, very finely chopped

2 cloves garlic, very finely chopped

1½ cups bottled tomato ketchup

½ cup bottled chili sauce

4 tablespoons dark brown sugar

4 tablespoons lemon juice

1 tablespoon Worcestershire sauce

½ tablespoon hot pepper sauce, or to taste

Salt and freshly ground black pepper, to taste

1. To prepare the sauce, heat the oil in a saucepan over medium heat. Add the onion and garlic and cook, stirring occasionally, for 5–7 minutes, until softened. Stir in the remaining ingredients, lower the heat, and simmer, stirring frequently, for about 45 minutes, until the flavors blend and the sauce is slightly thickened. Taste and adjust the seasoning, if necessary.

2. Put the ribs in a nonmetallic bowl large enough to hold them in a single layer. Pour the sauce over and make sure the ribs are well coated. Cover and refrigerate for at least 2 hours or overnight.

3. Prepare an outside charcoal, gas, or electric grill, or preheat a broiler. Arrange the ribs on an oiled rack, or a greased foil-lined broiler pan. Cook for about 20 minutes for medium, turning the ribs regularly and basting with the remaining sauce. Serve hot or at room temperature with freshly cooked corn-on-the-cob.

A typical western "rig" with a high cantle in the back to prevent the rider from sliding off. This "California Saddle," invented around 1880, was designed for heavy roping and long, daily rides of 70 miles or more.

"SON-OF-A-BITCH STEW"

Makes 4–6 servings; makes 8 dumplings

Traditionally made with freshly slaughtered cow's innards, this stew is firmly placed in the folklore of life on the trail. If all the literature and cowboys' memoirs are to be believed, cow handlers from Texas to Canada jumped for joy as the heart, liver, spleen, kidneys, tongue, testicles ("prairie oysters"), and brains went straight from the carcass to a Dutch oven for all-day stewing. This modern version combines kidneys with stewing beef to make a succulent stew.

2 pounds boneless beef chuck, trimmed and cut into 2-inch cubes

2 tablespoons all-purpose flour

2 tablespoons beef drippings or vegetable oil

10 ounces ox or lamb kidneys, trimmed, cores removed, and chopped

1 large onion, chopped

2 cups beef stock

2 teaspoons Worcestershire sauce

One bunch fresh herbs, such as parsley, bay, and thyme, tied together

Salt and freshly ground black pepper, to taste

HERB DUMPLINGS

1½ cups all-purpose flour

1½ teaspoons baking powder

½ teaspoon salt

3 ounces beef suet, grated

1 tablespoon finely chopped fresh parsley

1 tablespoon snipped fresh thyme

Salt and freshly ground pepper, to taste

4–6 tablespoons milk

1. Place the beef in a bowl. Sprinkle in the flour and toss until coated. Set aside.

2. Heat the drippings or oil in a large flameproof casserole over medium heat. Add the beef cubes, in batches, and fry on all sides until browned. Remove each batch with a draining spoon as it is ready. Set aside. Add extra oil or drippings to the pan if necessary. Add the kidney cubes and fry until brown on all sides. Remove and place with the beef.

3. Stir in the onions and fry for 5–7 minutes, until softened.

4. Return the beef and kidneys to the pan. Stir in the stock, Worcestershire sauce, herbs, and salt and pepper. Bring to a boil, then lower the heat, cover, and simmer for 2 hours.

5. After 1¾ hours, prepare the herb dumplings. Sift the flour, baking powder, and salt into a large mixing bowl. Stir in the suet, parsley, thyme, and salt and pepper. Add the milk, tablespoon by tablespoon, stirring continuously until the mixture comes together to form a soft dough.

6. Remove the fresh herbs from the pot. Using 2 large spoons, drop 8 balls of the dumpling batter into the simmering stew. Re-cover and simmer for 15–20 minutes, until the dumplings are puffed up. Taste and adjust the seasoning.

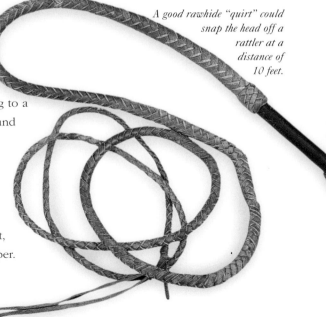

A good rawhide "quirt" could snap the head off a rattler at a distance of 10 feet.

CHARGRILLED SPATCHCOCKED GAME BIRDS

Makes 4 servings

Shooting wild game birds helped break up the monotony of a three-month-long cattle drive, as well as provide something other than beef and beans for meals. Prairie hens, sage hens, quail, and wild turkeys were plentiful. Guinea fowl or Cornish game hens make good substitutes.

2 guinea fowl or Cornish game hens, dressed

1 cup dry white wine

4 shallots or green onions (scallions), thinly sliced

2 sprigs fresh rosemary

BASTING SAUCE

½ cup vegetable oil

4 tablespoons shallot- or garlic-flavored vinegar

1 teaspoon Dijon mustard

Salt and freshly ground black pepper, to taste

1. To spatchcock the birds, working with one bird at a time, using a pair of kitchen scissors, cut along the length of the backbone on each side and remove it. Leave the rib cage whole. Turn the bird over and open it up. Flatten it by pressing down firmly. Spatchcock the remaining birds in the same way.

2. Place the birds in a glass dish large enough to hold them in a single layer. Pour the wine over. Sprinkle with the shallots or green onions (scallions) and rosemary, and leave to marinate in the refrigerator for at least 1 hour or up to 4 hours.

3. Meanwhile, to prepare the basting sauce, in a small bowl, mix together the oil, vinegar, and mustard. Season and set aside.

5. When ready to cook, prepare an outdoor charcoal, gas, or electric barbecue, or preheat the broiler.

5. Remove the birds from the marinade and discard the marinade. Pat each bird completely dry with paper towels. Stick 2 metal skewers diagonally through each bird to hold it flat while it cooks. Brush each bird liberally with the basting sauce.

6. Arrange the birds, skin side up, on an oiled rack, or on a greased foil-lined broiler pan, about 6 inches from the source of heat. Grill, basting frequently, for 30 minutes for the guinea fowl or 20 minutes for the game hens, turning the birds over frequently and basting with the remaining marinade, until the skin is crisp and the juices run clear when a thigh is pierced with the tip of a knife.

7. Wearing oven mitts or using pot holders, remove the skewers. Cut each bird in half and serve at once.

"BEAN HOLE" BEANS

Makes 4–6 servings

When there wasn't time to keep a constant eye on a pot of simmering beans, "Cookie," as many trail cooks were called, buried all the ingredients for a bean dish in a sealed can in the ground over hot coals, with more coals on top. The dried beans could then be left overnight or all day to become tender. This updated version of "bean-hole" cooking uses a flameproof casserole and includes fresh pumpkin, but other squash can be substituted.

1½ cups dried cannellini or pinto beans, soaked overnight, or 2 (16-ounce) cans cannellini or pinto beans, drained and rinsed

2 tablespoons vegetable oil

1½ large onions, chopped

3 large cloves garlic, chopped

2 (16-ounce) cans chopped tomatoes

2 teaspoons chopped fresh sage leaves, or 1 teaspoon rubbed sage

Hot pepper sauce, to taste

Freshly ground black pepper, to taste

3 cups peeled, seeded, and diced pumpkin (about 1 pound)

Salt, to taste

1. Drain and rinse the dried beans. Put them in a pot over high heat, cover with cold water, and bring to a boil. Boil for 10 minutes. Drain well.

2. Meanwhile, heat the oil in a flameproof casserole over medium heat. Add the onions and garlic and fry for 5–7 minutes, until softened.

3. Stir in the tomatoes and their juice, the sage leaves, hot pepper sauce, and pepper. Bring to a boil and boil for 5 minutes, stirring.

4. Add the cooked dried beans and pumpkin, lower the heat, cover, and simmer for about 1 hour, or until the beans are tender and the pumpkin is falling apart. If using canned beans, add the pumpkin to the pan and cook for 45 minutes, then stir in the beans. Taste and add salt. Serve at once.

BEEF STEAKS WITH FRIED ONIONS

Makes 4 servings

"Good old beef talking" was how retired cowboy Andy Adams described the sounds of sizzling steaks in The Log of a Cowboy, *his 1903 memories of his first cattle drive.[2] Any team bringing their herd into Kansas in the late spring would find small, wild onions, delicacies quickly added to the cook's simmering pots and skillets.*

2 tablespoons all-purpose flour

2 teaspoons dry mustard powder

1 teaspoon sugar

Salt and freshly ground black pepper, to taste

4 steaks, such as T-bones, 8–10 ounces and ½-inch thick each

2 tablespoons beef drippings (optional)

FRIED ONIONS

Vegetable oil for deep-frying

½ cup all-purpose flour

2 tablespoons cornstarch

1 teaspoon garlic salt

½ teaspoon dried thyme leaves

Freshly ground black pepper, to taste

1 large egg, lightly beaten

½ cup beer

2 large onions, halved and cut into ⅛-inch slices

Salt, to taste

1. Combine the 2 tablespoons of flour, mustard, sugar, and salt and pepper in a plastic bag and shake. Add the steaks, one at a time, shaking until lightly coated. Remove from the bag and shake any excess flour back into the bag. Discard any excess flour. Set aside the steaks.

2. Heat about 3 inches of vegetable oil for the fried onions in a large, deep skillet or wok over medium-high heat to a temperature of 350°F, or until a cube of bread browns in 30 seconds.

3. Meanwhile, to prepare the batter for the fried onions, sift the flour, cornstarch, garlic salt, thyme, and pepper into a bowl. Make a well in the middle and add the egg and beer. Use a fork to mix until just blended without beating. Do not worry if small amounts of flour remain visible in the batter.

4. Separate the onion slices. Using 2 forks and working in batches, quickly dip a few onions in the batter. Lift the onions out of the batter and shake off the excess. Drop them in the oil and fry for about 45 seconds, until pale golden and crisp.

5. Drain on paper towels. Transfer to a paper-towel-lined heatproof plate and sprinkle with salt. Keep warm in a low oven. Use a draining spoon to scoop any crusty bits out of the oil, and continue frying until all the onions and batter are used. Reheat the oil between batches.

6. Pour off all but 2 tablespoons of the oil in the skillet, or melt the beef drippings. Add the steaks to the pan and fry for 4 minutes on each side for rare, or 6 minutes on each side for well done. If all the steaks will not fit in the pan at once, fry in batches, keeping each fried steak warm in the oven until they are all fried. Add extra oil or drippings to the pan if necessary. Serve the steaks with the fried onions.

SKILLET-FRIED TROUT WITH HERB STUFFING

Makes 4 servings

Babbling mountain streams and crystal-clear lakes provided variation in a cowherder's diet with fresh fish, such as cutthroat, rainbow, and lake trout. When time was short, the fish were simply dressed and speared with long sticks for cooking over the campfire. If the cook was obliging, however, he would gather wild sage, thyme, and onions and pan-fry the fish in lard or beef drippings. Do not use dried herbs in this recipe.

4 trout, ¾–1 pound each, cleaned and dressed

8 thin onion slices

2 green onions (scallions), very finely chopped

Fresh herb leaves, such as thyme, tarragon, parsley, coriander (cilantro), dill, or mint, or a mixture

Salt and freshly ground black pepper, to taste

1 egg, lightly beaten

¼ cup yellow cornmeal

About 2 tablespoons butter

About 2 tablespoons vegetable oil

Lemon wedges, to serve

1. Rinse each trout inside and out and pat dry with paper towels. Place equal amounts of onion slices, green onions (scallions), and herbs inside each trout. Season generously with salt and pepper. Use wooden toothpicks to close each trout so the flavorings do not fall out during frying.

2. Place the egg in a shallow dish. Place the cornmeal in another shallow dish or plate and season with salt and pepper.

Dip the trout, one at a time, first in the egg and then in the cornmeal to coat evenly. Gently shake off any excess cornmeal from the trout.

3. Melt 1 tablespoon of butter with 1 tablespoon of oil in a large skillet over medium heat. Add the trout and fry for 3–4 minutes on each side, until the flesh flakes easily when tested with the tip of a knife. If all the trout will not fit in the pan at once, fry in batches and keep warm in a low oven. Add more butter and oil to the pan if necessary.

4. Serve the trout with lemon wedges for squeezing over the fish.

A good storm lantern made sure cowboys could see their coffee early in the morning. Cooks were doubly careful to keep the lantern glass from cracking while the chuck wagon creaked along.

CHUCK WAGON PORK 'N' BEANS

Makes 4–6 servings

Beans were one of the staples of a trail diet—eaten morning, noon, and night. In everyday trail parlance, they were called "prairie strawberries" and "whistle berries." Historian Ramon F. Adams wrote that one cowherder had his own name for them: " 'Deceitful beans—'cause they talk behind your back'." [5]

1½ cups dried pinto beans, soaked overnight, or 2 (16-ounce) cans pinto beans, drained and rinsed

2 tablespoons vegetable oil

2 pounds thick pork belly, cut into 2-inch chunks

2 large cloves garlic, crushed

1 red bell pepper, cored, seeded, and chopped

1 fresh jalapeño pepper, seeded and finely chopped

1 large onion, chopped

2 tablespoons tomato paste

1 (16-ounce) can chopped tomatoes

Vegetable stock or water (optional)

3 tablespoons dark brown sugar

1 tablespoon Worcestershire sauce

Salt and freshly ground black pepper, to taste

Hot pepper sauce (optional)

1. Drain and rinse the dried beans, if using. Put them in a saucepan over high heat, cover with cold water, and bring to a boil. Boil for 10 minutes. Drain well.

2. Meanwhile, heat the oil in a large flameproof casserole over medium heat.

Add the pork belly and fry, stirring, for about 5 minutes, until browned.

3. Add the garlic, bell pepper, jalapeño pepper, and onion and continue cooking, stirring, for about 5 minutes longer, until just softened.

4. Stir in the tomato paste, tomatoes with their juice, the cooked dried beans, if using, and enough vegetable stock or water to cover. Bring to a boil, then lower the heat, cover the pan, and simmer gently for about 45 minutes, stirring the mixture occasionally.

5. Stir in the sugar, Worcestershire sauce, and salt and pepper. Add the canned beans, if using. Add several drops of hot pepper sauce for a hot, spicy mixture. Leave the pot uncovered and continue to simmer for 15 minutes, until the beans are very tender.

BUFFALO STEAKS WITH WILD MUSHROOM SAUCE

Makes 4 servings

Native Americans had always valued the huge buffalo as a food source, and cowboys were quick to develop a taste for the lean meat. It naturally partnered the wild mushrooms found in northern woodlands. Today, buffalo is farmed and the meat is sold by specialist butchers and mail-order suppliers. Beef or venison steaks can be substituted.

4 buffalo filet steaks, about 4 ounces each, well trimmed

1 cup full-flavored red wine

1 teaspoon cracked black peppercorns

1 dried bay leaf, torn in half

2 tablespoons butter

WILD MUSHROOM SAUCE

1 cup Madeira wine

4 tablespoons butter

1 small onion, very finely chopped

5 cups thinly sliced wild mushrooms, such as ceps, shiitake, or morelles, or a mixture (about 1 pound)

2 cups beef or vegetable stock

Pinch of freshly grated nutmeg

Salt and freshly ground pepper, to taste

1. Place the buffalo steaks in a shallow, glass bowl large enough to hold them in a single layer. Pour the wine over, and add the black peppercorns and bay leaf. Cover and marinate at room temperature for at least 45 minutes, or up to 2 hours.

2. Meanwhile, to prepare the sauce, put the Madeira wine in a small saucepan over high heat and bring to a boil. Boil until reduced by half. Remove from the heat and set aside.

3. Melt the butter in a skillet over medium heat. Add the onions and fry, stirring, for 5–7 minutes, until softened. Add the mushrooms and continue cooking until the moisture they give off almost evaporates. Stir in the stock, reduce the heat to low, and simmer, uncovered, for 20 minutes, until reduced slightly.

Stir in the Madeira wine. Add the nutmeg, simmer for 15 minutes, then season.

4. Meanwhile, preheat the oven on a low setting. Remove the steaks from the marinade and pat dry with paper towels. Melt the butter in a large skillet over medium-high heat. Add the steaks and fry for 1 minute on each side for rare, or 2½ minutes for well done. If all the steaks will not fit in the pan at once, fry in batches and keep warm in the oven.

5. Serve the steaks with the mushroom sauce spooned alongside.

TRAILBLAZING BEEF STEW

Makes 4–6 servings

Meat from cattle herded for hundreds of miles before being slaughtered was tough and stringy, requiring slow simmering to become tender. Simple but hearty stews such as this were made all along the cattle routes, with each cook varying the ingredients depending on his stocks. For an authentic on-the-trail flavor, replace some or all of the stock with dark, black coffee.

2 pounds boneless beef chuck, trimmed and cut into 2-inch cubes

2 tablespoons all-purpose flour

Vegetable oil or beef drippings

2 onions, thinly sliced

1 clove garlic, chopped

4 cups beef stock or water, boiling

1 teaspoon Worcestershire sauce

2 sprigs fresh thyme leaves, or ½ tablespoon dried

1 dried bay leaf

Salt and ground black pepper, to taste

4 large carrots, cut into large chunks

1. Place the beef cubes in a bowl. Sprinkle in the flour and toss until lightly coated. Set aside.

2. Heat 2 tablespoons of vegetable oil or drippings in a large flameproof casserole over medium heat. Add the beef cubes, in batches, and fry on all sides until browned. Remove each batch with a draining spoon as it is ready. Set aside. Add extra oil or drippings if necessary.

3. Add the onions and garlic. Lower the heat, cover, and fry the onions for 5–7 minutes, until softened. Return the beef to the pan.

4. Stir in the stock, Worcestershire sauce, thyme, bay leaf, and salt and pepper. Bring to a boil, then lower the heat,

On the trail, the kitchen often moved twice a day. This durable enamel pot signaled that the kitchen was open, and food was on its way along with the coffee.

Trail cowboys insisted on strong, black coffee—and lots of it! "Cookie" would add an egg to the coffee pot, to help settle the grounds.

cover, and simmer for 2 hours, until the meat is almost tender. Add the carrots and continue simmering for about 30 minutes longer, until the vegetables are tender.

5. Taste and adjust the seasoning if necessary. Serve at once.

☙ BRUNSWICK STEW ☙

Makes 4–6 servings

After the Civil War, ex-Confederate soldiers headed for Texas to make a new life in the expanding cattle industry. Many became cooks, adapting traditional Southern specialties such as this stew to the wild game found along the trails.

1 stewing chicken, 3–4 pounds

1 rabbit, skinned, dressed, and cut up

Salt and freshly ground black pepper

1 large onion, chopped

2 large potatoes, about 8 ounces each, peeled and diced

1 (16-ounce) can chopped tomatoes

1 (16-ounce) can corn kernels, drained

1¾ cups fresh lima beans, or 1 (16-ounce) can lima beans, drained and rinsed

1 tablespoon light brown sugar

1 tablespoon Worcestershire sauce

1 tablespoon fresh thyme leaves, or ½ tablespoon dried

6 tablespoons butter or margarine

Hot pepper sauce

1. Place the chicken, rabbit pieces, and enough water to cover in a large flameproof casserole over high heat. Bring to a boil, skimming all gray foam from the surface. Stir in 2 tablespoons of salt, lower the heat, and poach, uncovered, for about 1 hour, or until the chicken is tender and the rabbit is cooked through and falling off the bones. Skim the surface as necessary.

2. Remove the chicken and rabbit pieces from the pan. Set aside. Remove all but 1 quart of the poaching liquid; the remainder can be used in other recipes or discarded. When the chicken and rabbit are cool enough to handle, remove all the meat from the bones and cut it into bite-size pieces. Discard the skins, cartilages, and bones.

3. Add the onion to the reserved poaching liquid and bring to a boil. Boil for 3 minutes to soften.

4. Lower the heat and return the chicken and rabbit meat to the pan. Stir in the potatoes, tomatoes with the juice, the corn, lima beans, brown sugar, Worcestershire sauce, and thyme. Season generously with salt and pepper.

5. Simmer, uncovered, over medium heat, stirring frequently, for about 45 minutes, until the liquid is reduced and the stew's consistency is like a chowder. The vegetables will be tender and the smallest pieces of meat will fall apart. The exact cooking time will depend on the size of the pan you are using.

6. Stir in the butter or margarine and adjust the seasoning. Serve at once with a bottle of hot pepper sauce for adding to individual portions.

🐎 BARBECUED VENISON HAUNCH 🐎

Makes 6–8 servings

On cattle drives, large wild game such as venison, antelope, and buffalo were plentiful and often shot for the pot. Lean, dense venison meat requires slow cooking to prevent it drying out. This recipe marinates the meat and grills it in tightly wrapped foil to preserve tenderness.

1 venison haunch, about 6 pounds, skinned and boned

Vegetable or olive oil, for brushing

Tex-Mex Cranberry Salsa (page 76), to serve

COOKED GAME MARINADE

½ bottle full-bodied red wine

4 tablespoons olive oil

1 tablespoon red wine vinegar

1 large carrot, peeled and chopped

1 large onion, sliced

1 clove garlic, sliced

1 teaspoon salt

1 fresh bay leaf, torn in half

1 bunch fresh herbs, such as parsley, thyme, and rosemary, tied together

8 juniper berries, lightly crushed

8 black peppercorns, lightly crushed

1. A day ahead, prepare the marinade. Place the wine, olive oil, vinegar, carrot, onion, garlic, and salt in a saucepan over high heat. Bring to a boil, skimming the surface. Lower the heat, stir in the remaining ingredients, and simmer, uncovered, for 15 minutes. Remove from the heat and leave to cool.

2. Open out the venison so it is flat, cutting the flesh if necessary. Put in a glass dish and pour the marinade over. Cover and leave to marinate overnight in the refrigerator. Return to room temperature before grilling.

3. The next day, prepare an outside charcoal, gas, or electric barbecue. Position the rack 6 inches above the heat.

4. Remove the venison from the marinade. Place on a double thickness of heavy-duty foil large enough to enclose the meat. Bring up the edges of the foil. Spoon 1 cup of the marinade over. Seal the foil so none of the juices can leak out

5. Place the foil package on the rack and grill for 45 minutes, turning over every 8 minutes. Remove the package from the rack and reposition the grid at its highest level. Brush the rack with oil.

6. Remove the meat from the foil, carefully reserving all the juices. Place it on the rack for 5 minutes, turning it over twice, to brown. Pour the juices into a small pan and bring to the boil for 3 minutes on the side of the rack or on the stovetop. Transfer the meat to a platter and let rest for 5 minutes. Slice thinly and spoon some marinade over. Accompany with the salsa.

SPOTTED PUP

Makes 4–6 servings

Historians record that old-fashioned rice puddings studded with raisins or other dried fruit and occasionally spiced with cinnamon were popular trail desserts. When sugar was not available, the puddings were sweetened with molasses, commonly called "lick." Cream adds a richness to this version trail riders would not have known.

1 quart milk

¾ cup dried cherries, raisins, or golden raisins

1 tablespoon finely grated orange zest

1 piece cinnamon stick, about 1½ inches long

1 cup short-grain rice

1 cup heavy cream

⅓ cup sugar

½ teaspoon vanilla extract

Pinch of salt

Maple syrup or molasses, to serve (optional)

1. Place the milk, dried fruit, orange zest, and cinnamon in a saucepan over medium heat. Bring just to a boil and stir in the rice.

2. Lower the heat and simmer, uncovered, stirring frequently, for 20 minutes, until the mixture thickens and the rice is almost tender. Stir in the cream, sugar, vanilla, and salt. Continue simmering for about 10 minutes, until the rice and fruit are tender and the mixture is thick and creamy.

3. Spoon the pudding into individual dishes to serve, topped with maple syrup or molasses, if desired. This can be served hot, at room temperature, or chilled.

Keeping milk cool often turned into a chance to make butter, or at least buttermilk. In the pioneer tradition, milk rocked in a milk cooler as the chuck wagon moved along would turn into clabber, then butter—a tasty campfire addition to pancakes.

WILD BERRY COBBLER

Makes 4–6 servings

When cowboys found wild berries or plum thickets along the trail, the fruit was collected and given to the cook to use in pies and cobblers—probably a welcomed variation from the regular fried dough, suet-filled desserts. Trail cooks "baked" their cobblers in a Dutch oven over hot coals, but a baking dish or soufflé dish is more appropriate today.

Butter, for greasing

5 cups mixed fresh berries, such as blackberries, raspberries, hulled and sliced strawberries, and red currants

2 tablespoons soft light brown sugar or granulated sugar

1 tablespoon finely grated orange zest

½ tablespoon cornstarch

½ teaspoon ground cinnamon

¼ teaspoon salt

Freshly ground black pepper (optional)

Vanilla ice cream, to serve (optional)

COBBLER TOPPING

1¾ cups all-purpose flour

1 tablespoon baking powder

1 tablespoon sugar

½ teaspoon salt

5 tablespoons butter or vegetable shortening, chilled and diced

¾ cup milk

1. Heat the oven to 425°F. Lightly grease an 8-inch round baking dish that is suitable for serving from. To prepare the filling, place the berries in a saucepan over medium heat. Add the sugar, orange zest, cornstarch, cinnamon, and salt. If the berry mixture includes strawberries, add a little black pepper, if you desire. Simmer, stirring gently, until the sugar dissolves. Bring to a boil. Turn off the heat, but cover the pan to keep the filling hot.

2. Meanwhile, to prepare the topping, sift the flour, baking powder, sugar, and salt into a bowl. Cut in the butter or shortening until the mixture forms coarse crumbs. Make a well in the middle, pour in the milk, and stir until a soft dough forms.

3. Spoon the hot filling into the prepared dish. Using lightly floured fingers, break off pieces of the dough and place them all over the surface so it is covered. Press down lightly so the mounds of dough are touching. Bake for 20–25 minutes, until the topping is golden and the filling is bubbling. Serve with vanilla ice cream on the side, if desired.

SON-OF-A-BITCH-IN-A-SACK

Makes 4–6 servings

Boiled suet puddings were popular chuck wagon desserts because they could be made from standard, non-perishable ingredients —flour, water, and dried fruit, along with ever-plentiful beef suet. On a generously funded drive, sorghum molasses, or "lick," was poured over the top, or occasionally the dessert would be served with stewed wild berries picked along the trail. The coffee-flavored sauce in this recipe replaces the molasses or berries.

1½ cups all-purpose flour

1½ teaspoons baking powder

1 teaspoon salt

2 tablespoons finely grated orange or lemon zest

3 ounces beef suet, grated

½ cup raisins or golden raisins

HOT COFFEE CUSTARD SAUCE

4 egg yolks

3 tablespoons vanilla-flavored sugar

2 cups milk, simmering

2 tablespoons strong black, cold coffee

1. Preheat the oven to 350°F.

2. Sift the flour, baking powder, and salt into a large mixing bowl. Stir in the orange or lemon zest until evenly distributed, then stir in the suet and raisins or golden raisins. Add ½ cup cold water and stir until a light dough forms. Add extra water, tablespoon by tablespoon, if necessary. Turn out the dough on a lightly floured surface and roll it into a thick, 9-inch log.

3. Place a wire rack in a roasting pan on top of 4 upturned ramekins so it does not sit on the bottom. Place the pudding on top. Pour enough boiling water into the pan to come to the bottom of the pudding. Cover the pan with a large sheet of foil, crimping it all around the edge so steam can not escape during baking.

4. Bake on the middle shelf of the oven for 1 hour, or until the pudding is slightly swollen and set.

5. Meanwhile, prepare the sauce. Place the eggs and sugar in a large heatproof bowl and beat with a wooden spoon until pale and creamy. Pour in the milk, whisking constantly. Pour the mixture into the top of a double boiler over simmering water. Stir constantly for about 20 minutes, until the sauce thickens and coats the back of the spoon. Remove from the heat and stir in the coffee. Serve warm with the pudding.

At the Ranch & Trailhead

EGGS 'N' HASH

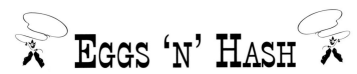

Makes 4–6 servings

The most significant change in cowboys' diets when meals moved from the back of wagons in the open to ranch cookhouses was the inclusion of eggs. Before the end of the last century, the XIT Ranch, the largest in the West, provided daily meals of "ham, eggs, and even butter, a chuck wagon diet undreamed of before the coming of the XIT." [1]

About 4 tablespoons vegetable oil or bacon fat

4 green onions (scallions), chopped

2 red bell peppers, halved, cored, and cut into ½-inch dice

2 green bell peppers, halved, cored, and cut into ½-inch dice

2 large potatoes, about 8 ounces each, peeled and cut into ½-inch dice

Salt and freshly ground black pepper, to taste

2 cups diced corned or plain cooked beef, cut into ½-inch dice

½ tablespoon paprika

1 tablespoon fresh thyme leaves, or ½ tablespoon dried

4–6 large eggs

½ cup chopped fresh parsley or coriander (cilantro)

Hot pepper or Worcestershire sauce, to serve (optional)

1. Heat the oil in a large, deep skillet with a tight-fitting lid over medium heat. Add the green onions (scallions), red and green bell peppers, potatoes, and salt and pepper and fry, stirring often, for about 8 minutes, until the potatoes are crispy on the outside and tender when pierced with the tip of a knife. Be careful not to break up the potatoes. Add a little extra oil or fat to the pan, if necessary.

2. Stir in the beef, paprika, and thyme and warm through. Taste and adjust the seasoning. Reduce the heat to low.

3. Using the back of a wooden spoon, make an indentation for each egg in the top of the hash. Break an egg into each indentation.

4. Cover the skillet and cook the eggs for about 10 minutes, until set but still soft in the middle, or to taste. Sprinkle with the chopped parsley or coriander (cilantro). Serve at once, straight from the skillet, with hot pepper sauce or Worcestershire sauce for sprinkling over individual portions, if desired.

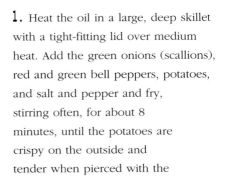

PORK 'N' HERB SAUSAGE PATTIES

Makes about 12 patties

Cow hands demand a filling breakfast as much today as they did during the 1880s and 1890s. The sausage mixture for these flavorful patties can be mixed a day in advance and refrigerated until it is time to fry them in the morning. Serve these with crisp bacon, hash browns, or Irish "Camp Potatoes" (page 42).

1½ pounds lean ground pork

½ cup fresh fine whole-wheat bread crumbs

1 large egg, lightly beaten

1 green onion (scallion), white part only, finely chopped

2 teaspoons very finely chopped fresh sage leaves, or 1 teaspoon rubbed sage

2 tablespoons very finely chopped fresh parsley

¼ teaspoon ground nutmeg

Salt and freshly ground black pepper, to taste

Vegetable oil, bacon fat, or beef drippings, for frying

1. Put the pork, bread crumbs, egg, green onion (scallion), sage, parsley, nutmeg, and salt and pepper into a large bowl. Gently mix until combined.

2. Shape the mixture into 12 patties, each about 2½ inches across. If the mixture is too sticky, lightly flour your hands. Cover the patties and chill for at least 30 minutes, or up to 24 hours.

3. If you do not have a nonstick skillet large enough to fry all the patties at once, use 2 skillets.

4. Heat 1 tablespoon of oil, fat, or drippings in a large nonstick skillet over medium heat. Add as many patties as will fit and fry for about 25 minutes, turning them over once, until the meat is cooked through and the outsides are slightly crispy. Drain the patties on paper towels and keep warm in the oven until they are all are fried.

A typical day's trail ride of 25–70 miles was through waterless, rock-dry desert terrain. No cowboy would leave camp without a supply of water tied to the saddle, no matter how saline or brackish the water tasted.

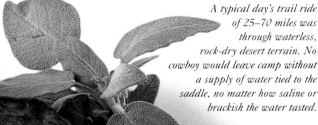

39

BLUEBERRY SADDLE BLANKETS

Makes about fourteen 4-inch pancakes

"Saddle blankets" and "splatter dabs" were two trail terms for pancakes or griddle cakes that remained in common use on ranches into this century. Maple syrup may be synonymous with pancakes today, but early cowboys would have eaten these pancakes with sorghum molasses, honey, or cane syrup.

1¼ cups all-purpose flour

½ teaspoon baking powder

½ teaspoon baking soda

Pinch of salt

¾ cup buttermilk

½–¾ cup milk

1 tablespoon honey

1 tablespoon butter, melted

¼ teaspoon vanilla extract

½ cup fresh blueberries

Vegetable oil for brushing

Butter and maple syrup, to serve

1. Stir together the flour, baking powder, baking soda, and salt in a large mixing bowl. Make a well in the middle.

2. Beat together the buttermilk, ½ cup milk, honey, melted butter, and vanilla extract. Pour the liquid ingredients into the dry ingredients and stir until just combined, adding a little extra milk if necessary. Do not worry if small amounts of flour remain visible in the mixture. Stir in the blueberries.

3. Place a large skillet or griddle with a nonstick surface over medium heat and very lightly brush with oil. Drop the batter by spoonfuls on to the hot skillet or griddle and cook for about 45 seconds, until the

Supplies for range-riding were stored in these ample leather pouches that hung on either flank—beans, bread, jerked meat, a flask of whiskey, and sometimes a Bible.

edges of the pancakes look set and the top is filled with bubbles.

4. Turn the pancakes over and cook for about 30 seconds longer, until golden on the bottom. Transfer to a plate and keep warm in the oven.

5. Continue making pancakes until all the batter is used. Serve hot, topped with butter and with maple syrup for pouring over the tops.

Variation

SOURDOUGH BLUEBERRY SADDLE BLANKETS Replace the milk with ½ cup of Sourdough Starter (page 66), at room temperature, and follow the recipe above. If the batter is too thick to fall from the spoon, add extra buttermilk, tablespoon by tablespoon. (Leave the starter at room temperature overnight if you plan to make these for breakfast. Replenish the starter left in the covered container in the refrigerator with ⅓ cup of all-purpose flour and 4 tablespoons of water.)

IRISH "CAMP POTATOES"

Makes 4–6 servings

One of the few potato dishes cowboys ever ate was called "camp potatoes"—a simple mixture of bacon and potatoes cooked in water. This version of creamy potatoes and peppers reflects the influence of Irish immigrants' cooking in cow-town kitchens and on ranches. It is similar to an Irish dish called Potatoes O'Brien.

1 cup half-and-half

2 pounds baking potatoes, such as Idahos, peeled and cut into ¼-inch dice

2 large red, green, orange, or yellow bell peppers, cored, seeded, and finely chopped

6 green onions (scallions), finely chopped

1 tablespoon all-purpose flour

1 cup finely shredded Monterey Jack or sharp cheddar cheese

½ cup finely chopped fresh parsley

Cayenne pepper, to taste

Salt and freshly ground black pepper, to taste

1½ tablespoons butter

1. Preheat the oven to 400°F. Lightly grease an 8-inch round baking dish.

2. Place the half-and-half in a saucepan over medium heat and bring to a simmer. When small bubbles appear around the edge, remove from the heat. Set aside.

3. Meanwhile, place the potatoes, bell peppers, and green onions (scallions) in the baking dish and toss together. Sprinkle the flour over and toss again. Add the cheese, parsley, cayenne pepper, and salt and pepper. Toss the ingredients again.

4. Pour in the warm half-and-half. Dot the top with the butter.

5. Bake for about 1 hour, stirring after 30 minutes, until the surface is golden and the potatoes feel tender when pierced with the tip of a knife. Serve at once.

Refitting stirrups, quirts, and other equipment often demanded a strand of horsehair. Handy clippers kept the horse well trimmed.

CORNMEAL-TOPPED CHILI

Makes 4–6 servings

Chili con carne is associated with the traditional images of cowboy life, and is still a popular dish in ranch dining rooms. The simple cornmeal topping on this easy and filling dish is a good foil for the hotness of the chili. There isn't any need to serve a potato with this. A lightly cooked green vegetable, or carrots, is ideal.

1 quantity Chili con Carne (page 14)

½ tablespoon hot pepper sauce, or to taste (optional)

Vegetable oil for brushing

Extra sharp cheddar, Parmesan, or Monterey Jack cheese

CORNMEAL COBBLER TOPPING

1¼ cups milk

Salt and freshly ground black pepper, to taste

Freshly grated nutmeg

½ cup yellow cornmeal

1 egg, lightly beaten

6 tablespoons finely shredded sharp cheddar, Parmesan, or Monterey Jack cheese

1. To prepare the cornmeal topping, lightly grease a baking sheet. Put the milk in a saucepan over high heat and bring to a boil. Add salt, pepper, and nutmeg to taste. Sprinkle in the cornmeal and stir constantly until the mixture becomes so thick the spoon is able to stand up in it. Remove the pan from the heat and stir in the egg and cheese.

2. Pour the cornmeal mixture onto the prepared baking sheet and use a metal spatula to spread it out into a rectangle ½-inch thick. Set aside for about 30 minutes, or until set and cool.

3. Meanwhile, preheat the oven to 350°F. Place the Chili con Carne in a saucepan over medium heat and reheat until it is almost boiling. Stir in the hot pepper sauce, if using. Transfer to a 9-inch square baking dish that is suitable for serving from.

4. When the cornmeal topping is cool, using a 1½-inch round biscuit cutter, cut out about 15 circles, cutting them as close together as possible.

5. Break up and sprinkle the cornmeal trimmings around the edge the chili. Decoratively arrange the circles over the top, overlapping them.

6. Lightly brush the top of each cornmeal circle with oil. Grate a little extra cheese over the chili and topping. Bake for about 20 minutes, until the chili and topping are heated through and the topping is golden brown. Serve at once straight from the dish.

SEA PLUM FRITTERS

Makes about 24 fritters

Canned oysters, fresh eggs, and ice cream were some of the luxuries on hotel menus when a range rider got to a cow town at the end of a cattle drive. "Sea plums" was one of the names cow hands used for oysters, and "soft grub" was how they described hotel food.
Serve these light, silver-dollar-looking fritters as a first course with salad leaves dressed with a lemon-flavored dressing.

18 fresh oysters, shucked, or 24 canned smoked oysters, drained, chopped

6 tablespoons all-purpose flour

6 tablespoons milk

6 eggs, separated

2 tablespoons finely grated lemon zest

½ teaspoon dried dillweed

Salt and freshly ground black pepper, to taste

Butter and vegetable oil, for frying

Lemon wedges, to garnish

1. Pat the oysters dry with paper towels and set aside. To prepare the batter, place the flour in a mixing bowl and make a well in the middle. Beat in the milk, egg yolks, lemon zest, dillweed, and salt and pepper. Stir in the oysters.

2. In a separate bowl, using perfectly clean beaters, beat the egg whites until stiff peaks form. Using a rubber spatula or a large metal spoon, fold the whites into the oyster mixture.

3. Melt 1 teaspoon of butter and 1 teaspoon of oil in a large nonstick skillet over medium heat and swirl to coat the bottom. Drop the batter in 2-tablespoon mounds onto the skillet and fry for about

1 minute, until the edges look set and the top is filled with bubbles. Turn the fritters over and cook for about 30 seconds longer, or until golden on the bottoms. Transfer to a plate and place in a low oven to keep warm.

4. Continue making fritters until all the batter is used, adding extra butter and oil if necessary. Transfer to a serving platter and serve, garnished with lemon wedges for squeezing over.

By 1860, the true cowboy boot had a higher heel, designed to stay in the stirrup, along with fancy stitching in its soft leather top.

Spurs were vital to the tough cowboy image, as well as being useful to flick his horse into startled motion. Fancy silver spurs were for dress; plain ones were for everyday, round-up work. Note the spiked rowell attached to the spur shank.

46

OXTAIL STEW

Makes 4–6 servings

Good husbandry on a ranch meant no edible part of an animal was wasted. Although oxtails have fallen from favor, they have rich and succulent meat. This old-fashioned recipe is made with beef stock and wine, but it can also be made with all stock. Serve with Hasselback Spuds (page 45), Golden Mashed Potatoes (page 56), or lightly boiled broccoli. Alternatively, make the dumplings on page 18 and add them to the stew for the final 15–20 minutes' cooking.

3 pounds thick, meaty oxtail pieces

2 tablespoons vegetable oil or beef drippings

2 large cloves garlic, crushed

2 large onions, thinly sliced

3 cups beef stock

1 cup dry red wine, such as pinot noir

2 dried bay leaves

2 carrots, peeled and sliced

2 parsnips, peeled, cored, and sliced

Salt and freshly ground black pepper, to taste

TOPPING

½ cup finely chopped fresh parsley or coriander (cilantro)

1 large clove garlic, halved, green core removed, and finely chopped

4 tablespoons finely grated lemon zest

1. Preheat the oven to 425°F. Place the oxtail pieces in a roasting pan large enough to hold them in a single layer. Roast for 45 minutes, turning all the pieces over twice so they brown evenly and some of the fat drips off.

2. Meanwhile, heat the oil or drippings in a large flameproof casserole over a low heat. Stir in the garlic and onions, cover the pan, and sweat for about 20 minutes.

3. Using a draining spoon, transfer the pieces of oxtail to the pan with the onions, leaving behind as much fat as possible. Stir in the beef stock, wine, and bay leaves. Bring to a boil. Lower the heat, cover, and simmer over low heat for 2½ hours.

4. Meanwhile, to prepare the topping, place the parsley or coriander (cilantro), garlic, and lemon zest on a chopping board and chop until fine and well combined. Set aside.

5. Add the carrots and parsnips to the pan and continue simmering for about 20 minutes, until tender-crisp. Season the stew with salt and pepper. Sprinkle with the topping and serve at once.

ALL-DAY SPICED BRISKET

Makes 6–8 servings

Even if cooking on a ranch is easier than on the trail—without any worries about heat sources or food spoiling—a cowboy cook's day has always been busy, once regularly beginning several hours before sunrise. Here is a flavorful dish that can be put in the oven and forgotten about for hours—ideal for all busy cooks.

1 boneless rolled brisket, about 4 pounds

1 tablespoon honey, melted

2 fresh bay leaves

Salt and freshly ground black pepper, to taste

SPICY HOT RUB

2 teaspoons ground cinnamon

2 teaspoons ground cumin

1 teaspoon ground coriander

1 teaspoon cayenne pepper, or to taste

1. Up to 24 hours before cooking, prepare the rub. Mix together the cinnamon, cumin, coriander, and cayenne pepper. Rub the brisket all over with the honey, then rub all over with the dry mixture. Place the meat on a double thickness of foil large enough to enclose it, then slide the bay leaves into the rolls in the brisket. Fold over the foil, making sure all the seams are securely sealed. Refrigerate until required.

2. Remove the meat from the refrigerator 30 minutes before cooking so it comes to room temperature; do not open the foil. Preheat the oven to 225°F. Line a roasting pan with a layer of foil.

3. Place the meat in the pan and roast for 5 hours, until the meat feels soft when pressed through the foil. Remove from the oven and leave to rest for 20 minutes before slicing.

4. To serve, unwrap the meat. Transfer any juices accumulated in the foil to a saucepan over medium heat and reheat.

5. Taste and add salt and pepper. Remove the bay leaves, slice thinly, and serve with the cooking juices spooned over.

A lariat of braided rawhide had to be strong enough to throw a 1,200-pound steer. The consummate cowhand could throw his 40-foot lasso with surprising accuracy, catching a steer by the hoof or horn.

PLANKED SALMON

Makes 8–10 servings

Cooking fish on an plank of wood over hot coals was a technique cowboys learned from Native Americans. It produces a slightly crisp exterior with succulent flesh. Use a nontreated hardwood board large enough to hold the fish with a 1½ to 2-inch border all around. Fruitwoods, such as apple or cherry, or cedar and oak are ideal. Hammer nails at 2-inch intervals into the thin edges on both sides; leave enough of the nail heads extended to wrap thin wire around them.

3 tablespoons sunflower oil

Handful fresh herb leaves, such as sorrel, mint, dill, or tarragon

1 large salmon fillet, about 2½ pounds, unskinned

Sorrel Sauce (page 76), to serve

LEMON RUB

2 tablespoons finely grated lemon zest

1 teaspoon salt

1 teaspoon ground black pepper

½ teaspoon dry mustard powder

1. Prepare the plank (see above).

2. To prepare the lemon rub, in a small bowl, mix together the lemon zest, salt, pepper, and mustard powder. Set aside.

3. Prepare an outdoor charcoal or gas barbecue. Brush one side of the plank with 1 tablespoon of the oil. Place the wood, oiled-side down, directly onto the coals or the rack until it is throughly charred. Remove the plank and brush the charred side with another tablespoon of oil. Stack a pile of bricks on each side of the rack, slightly less than the distance of the plank apart and with one side one brick shorter than the other. The tallest stack should be about 6 inches above the source of heat.

4. Arrange the fresh herbs along the middle of the wood. Place the salmon on top, skin side down. Brush with the remaining oil and add the lemon rub.

5. Tie a piece of thin wire, about twice the length of the plank, to the nails on each side of the wood at one end. Crisscross the wires over the salmon fillet, securing them on the nails, as if lacing a shoe. Keep the wire taught.

6. Place the plank on the brick stacks, fish side down and with the tail end on the taller stack of bricks. Grill for 15–20 minutes, until the flesh is firm. If it starts to char, add a brick to each of the stacks.

7. Remove the plank from the heat. Use wire cutters to remove the wire. Cut the salmon into serving portions. Serve the sorrel sauce separately.

BEST-IN-THE-WEST RIBS

Makes 6 servings

When a roundup finished, it was time for big celebrations. All the hands from neighboring ranches were invited, and the ranch cook went all out to provide a spread that would be the talk of the ranges for weeks — nothing but the best would do. Dry-marinated and slowly grilled pork ribs like these, tender and juicy, were the order of the day. The barbecue sauce suggested in this recipe is mildly flavored. For a hotter sauce, use Sizzling Barbecue Sauce (page 16).

2 meaty country-style racks pork ribs, about 3 pounds each

Campfire BBQ Sauce (page 78)

GARLIC DRY RUB

2 tablespoons garlic salt

½ tablespoon paprika

½ tablespoon onion salt

½ tablespoon celery salt

½ tablespoon light brown sugar

1 teaspoon salt

½ teaspoon turmeric

½ teaspoon cayenne pepper, or to taste

Freshly ground black pepper, to taste

1. The day before cooking, prepare the garlic dry rub. In a small bowl, combine all the ingredients. Rub both racks of ribs all over with the dry rub until they are lightly coated. Wrap each rib in a double layer of heavy-duty aluminum foil, folding over all the ends so none of the juices can escape during grilling. Refrigerate the ribs overnight.

2. The next day, remove the ribs from the refrigerator and leave to come to room temperature. Meanwhile, prepare an outdoor charcoal, gas, or electric grill, or preheat an oven broiler.

3. Place the foil packages on the rack, about 6 inches from the source of the heat. Cook for 45 minutes, turning the packages over every 10–15 minutes and watching that the foil does not burn. Either make the barbecue sauce, or reheat it, and bring it to a boil.

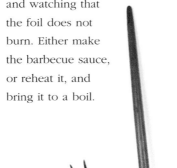

4. Unwrap the ribs and place them on the rack. Continue cooking for 30–40 minutes, turning them frequently and basting with the barbecue sauce, until cooked through and the juices run clear when pierced with the tip of a knife. Serve at once with any remaining sauce for dipping.

COOKHOUSE MEATLOAF

Makes 4–6 servings

Few collections of cowboy recipes do not include a version of the ever-popular meatloaf. Cold slices make a satisfying lunch with Sourdough Bread (page 69) and Chili Bread-and-Butter Pickles (page 77).

2 tablespoons vegetable oil

1 onion, chopped

12 ounces lean ground beef

12 ounces lean ground veal

1 large egg, lightly beaten

½ cup fresh whole-wheat bread crumbs

½ cup very finely chopped fresh parsley

¼ teaspoon ground allspice

Freshly grated nutmeg

Salt and freshly ground black pepper, to taste

4 tablespoons milk

4–6 tablespoons Sizzling Barbecue Sauce (page 16), to taste (optional)

4 slices unsmoked bacon

1. Preheat the oven to 350°F. Heat the oil in a skillet over medium heat. Add the onion and fry, stirring occasionally, for 5–7 minutes, until softened.

2. Meanwhile, place the beef, veal, egg, bread crumbs, parsley, allspice, a pinch of nutmeg, and salt and pepper into a bowl. Sprinkle the milk over the bread crumbs.

3. Add the onion and when cool enough to handle, using your hands, squeeze all the ingredients together until blended.

4. Transfer to a 9 x 5 x 2-inch bread pan and pat into the corners. Spread with the barbecue sauce for a spicy version. Arrange the bacon slices on top, covering as much of the surface as possible.

5. Bake for 1 hour, or until the juices run clear when a knife is inserted into the middle. Pour off the excess fat, then leave the meatloaf to stand for 5 minutes in the pan.

If necessary, run a round-bladed knife around the sides to loosen. Invert onto a plate, giving the pan a firm shake. Turn right side up and transfer to a serving platter. Serve at once.

BORDER TOMATO RICE

Makes 4–6 servings

Mexicans have always been cowboy cooks, and their style of cooking is a regular feature on many ranches today, especially those in the Southwest. This variation of **arroz rojos** *combines Mexican spices and cowboys' once-insatiable appetite for tomatoes. At one time, tomatoes, even though they were canned, were served three times a day—for breakfast, dinner (midday meal), and supper (evening meal).*

2 tablespoons vegetable oil

1¼ cups long-grain rice

1 onion, finely chopped

1 small red bell pepper, cored, seeded, and chopped

1 large clove garlic, finely chopped

½ teaspoon ground cumin

¼ teaspoon cayenne pepper, or to taste

2 large tomatoes, seeded and finely chopped

1¼ cups chicken or vegetable stock, boiling

Salt and freshly ground black pepper, to taste

Fresh sage leaves, to garnish

1. Heat a large heavy-bottomed skillet with a lid or a flameproof casserole over medium heat for 30 seconds. Add the vegetable oil and rice. Cook, stirring, for about 2 minutes, until the rice is coated and turning opaque.

2. Stir in the onion, bell pepper, and garlic and fry, stirring frequently, for 3 minutes. Stir in the cumin, cayenne pepper, and tomatoes and continue cooking, stirring gently, for about 1 minute.

3. Pour in the stock and bring to a boil. Season generously with salt and pepper. Lower the heat, cover, and simmer for 20 minutes, until the rice is tender and all the liquid absorbed. Remove the pan from the heat and fork the rice and vegetables onto a serving dish. Garnish with fresh sage leaves and serve at once.

SHEPHERD'S PIE

Makes 4–6 servings

A strong British presence in the large ranches existed at the end of the last century, with many of them being financed by London-based consortiums. English, Scottish, and Irish men also cooked on ranches, so it wasn't surprising the British influence extended to mealtimes. This English recipe, originally for using left-over beef and gravy, is ideal cookhouse fare because it is filling and easy to prepare.

2 tablespoons vegetable oil or beef drippings

1 large onion, chopped

1 pound cultivated mushrooms, such as crisimi, wiped and sliced

2 pounds lean ground beef

1 cup beef stock

Salt and freshly ground black pepper, to taste

1 tablespoon butter

GOLDEN MASHED POTATOES

1 pound white potatoes, peeled and chopped

1 pound sweet potatoes, peeled and chopped

½–¾ cup milk

4 tablespoons butter

Salt and freshly ground black pepper, to taste

Freshly grated nutmeg, to taste

1. To prepare the mashed potatoes, bring a large saucepan of salted water to a boil. Add the white and sweet potatoes and boil for about 15 minutes, or until very tender. Drain and leave in the colander to dry for a few minutes.

2. Transfer the potatoes to a large mixing bowl. Using a potato masher or an electric mixer, beat the potatoes until they are broken up. Add the milk and butter and continue mixing until smooth and fluffy. Season generously with salt and pepper, and nutmeg. Set aside.

3. Meanwhile, preheat the oven to 350°F. Heat the oil or drippings in a large flameproof casserole over medium heat. Add the onion and fry, stirring occasionally, for 5–7 minutes, until softened. Add the meat and stir it around until it starts to brown. Stir in the stock. Season to taste.

4. Transfer the meat mixture to a 9-inch square baking dish suitable for serving from. Attractively spoon or pipe the mashed potatoes over the top. Dot with butter.

5. Bake for 45 minutes, until the filling is piping hot and the topping is lightly golden. Serve at once, straight from the dish.

Chaps helped a cowboy withstand rope burns, rough riding, and even horse bites. Made of worked leather, these seatless coverings tied behind the leg for easy wearing.

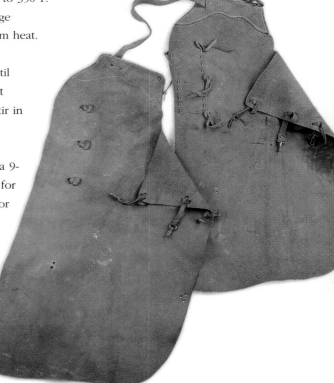

RANCHYARD CHICKEN 'N' DUMPLINGS

Makes 4–6 servings; makes 12 dumplings

As ranches became established, flocks of chickens were bred to provide meat and eggs for the cookhouse. This old-fashioned favorite is a complete meal in a pot. It's warming, filling, and substantial enough for hard-working ranch workers.

½ cup all-purpose flour

Salt and ground black pepper, to taste

1 broiler-fryer chicken, about 3½ pounds, cut into 8 pieces

Butter, for frying

Vegetable oil, for frying

4 large leeks, halved, rinsed, and sliced

2 onions, chopped

4 large carrots, peeled and sliced

2 celery stalks, sliced

Bunch of fresh herbs, such as parsley, thyme, and bay leaves, tied together

1 teaspoon celery seeds

1 quart chicken stock

PAPRIKA DUMPLINGS

2¼ cups all-purpose flour

2 teaspoons baking powder

1½ teaspoons salt

1 teaspoon paprika

3 tablespoons vegetable oil

¾–1 cup milk

1. Combine the flour and salt and pepper in a plastic bag. Add the chicken pieces, one at a time, shaking until lightly coated. Remove from the bag and shake any excess flour back into the bag.

2. Melt 2 tablespoons of butter with 1 tablespoon of oil in a large flameproof casserole over medium-high heat. Add as many chicken pieces as will fit in a single layer and fry for about 5 minutes on each sides until crisp and golden. Set aside. Continue until all the chicken pieces are fried, adding more butter and vegetable oil as necessary. Pour off all but 1 tablespoon of the melted fat.

3. Add the leeks and onions and cook for 5–7 minutes, stirring often, until softened. Add the carrots, celery, bunch of herbs, and celery seeds. Return all the chicken pieces to the pan and pour in the stock. Bring to a boil. Lower the heat, cover, and simmer for 10 minutes.

4. Meanwhile, prepare the dumplings. Sift the flour, baking powder, salt, and paprika into a large bowl. Make a well in the middle. Pour in the oil, then add ¾ cup of milk. Stir together to make a soft dough, adding extra milk, tablespoon by tablespoon, if necessary.

5. Uncover the pan and drop 12 spoonfuls of the batter on top of the simmering casserole. Continue simmering, uncovered, for 10 minutes. Cover the pan and simmer for 10 minutes longer, until the chicken is tender and the juices run clear when the thickest pieces are pierced and the dumplings are puffed up and cooked through. Serve at once.

PLUM DUFF

Makes 4–6 servings

Boiled dried fruit and suet pudding was a popular dessert throughout the West, not just on ranches. Today, this is called a plum pudding (the earliest versions contained dried plums, but now a mix of dried fruits is used) and usually only served at Christmas, but it makes a filling dessert for wintertime. "Duff" comes from an old English pronunciation of "dough."

⅔ cup seedless raisins

⅔ cup dried currants

⅔ cup golden raisins

5 tablespoons brandy or orange juice

6 ounces beef suet, shredded

2 jumbo eggs, lightly beaten

2 cups fresh white or whole-wheat bread crumbs

½ cup all-purpose flour, sifted

½ cup finely ground blanched almonds

½ cup packed light brown sugar

3 tablespoons chopped candied lemon peel

3 tablespoons chopped candied orange peel

1 teaspoon apple pie spice

Salt, to taste

Freshly grated nutmeg, to taste

Confectioner's sugar

Hot Coffee Custard Sauce (page 35), made without coffee

1. Place the dried fruit in a large bowl. Sprinkle with brandy or juice and leave for 20 minutes.

2. Stir in the remaining ingredients. Set aside, covered, for 12 hours.

3. Bring a large, deep saucepan half-filled with water to a boil. Fold a 1-yard square of cheesecloth in quarters and heavily flour the top layer. Spoon the duff batter into the middle of the cloth. Pull the cloth up around the batter and shape into a ball, rolling it on the countertop. Tightly tie with a long piece of string,

forming a tight mold. Wrap heavy-duty foil around the outside of the duff so it is completely enclosed.

4. Tie to a long-handled wooden spoon. Place the handle across the top of the pot, so the duff is suspended in the water but not touching the pan bottom. Add enough water so it is covered. Cover the pan tightly with foil. Boil for 8 hours, adding more boiling water as necessary.

5. Drain the water from the pan and leave the duff suspended for 4 hours to set.

6. Prepare the sauce. Remove the foil and cloth and transfer the duff to a serving dish. Sprinkle with the confectioner's sugar and serve with the sauce.

PLUM CRISP

Serves 4–6

An old-fashioned dessert that once would have been partnered with rich and creamy hand-churned ice cream. Serve this hot, or at room temperature, with whipped cream or store-bought premium ice cream.

Butter or margarine

1½ pounds plums, about 12, halved, pitted, and sliced

1 tablespoon arrowroot

⅓ cup packed light brown sugar

1½ tablespoons finely grated orange zest

½ tablespoon orange juice

1 cinnamon stick, about 3-inches long, broken into pieces

½ cup all-purpose flour

½ cup quick-cooking rolled oats

5 tablespoons sugar

½ cup unsalted chilled butter, diced

1. Preheat the oven to 375°F. Butter a 9-inch square or 10-inch round baking dish that is suitable for serving from.

2. Place the plums in the prepared dish. Sift over the arrowroot and gently toss the plums. Sprinkle the brown sugar and orange zest and juice over the fruit. Bury the cinnamon pieces in the plums.

3. In a mixing bowl, mix together the flour, oats, and sugar. Cut in the butter until coarse crumbs form. Sprinkle over the plums and press down lightly.

4. Bake for 35–40 minutes, until the topping is golden and crisp and the plums feel tender if pierced with the tip of a knife. Remove from the oven and leave for about 5 minutes before serving while the topping crisps.

OATMEAL PIE

Makes 8–10 slices

Freshly baked pies have always been a popular dessert in ranch dining rooms. With its rich and thick filling, this sweet pie is best in the winter. Serve with a dollop of ice cream.

2 large eggs

¾ cup honey

1 cup quick-cooking rolled oats

¾ cup light brown sugar, packed

½ cup butter or margarine, melted

¾ cup raisins or golden raisins

¾ cup chopped pecans

1 teaspoon ground cinnamon

2 tablespoons finely grated orange zest

Vanilla ice cream, to serve

PIECRUST

1¼ cups all-purpose flour

¼ cup self-rising flour

½ teaspoon salt

½ cup vegetable shortening or butter, or a mixture, chilled and diced

About 5 tablespoons iced water

1. Prepare the piecrust. Sift both the flours and salt into a mixing bowl. Cut in the shortening or butter until coarse crumbs form. Tossing with a fork, add the water, tablespoon by tablespoon, until a soft dough forms. The exact amount of water will depend on the absorbency of the flour.

2. Gather the dough into a ball. Roll out on a lightly floured countertop into a circle until it is about ⅛-inch thick and 11 inches across. Transfer to a 9-inch pie plate and trim the excess so there is a ½–inch overhang. Fold the underhang under and pinch to seal, then crimp all around. (Use the dough trimmings to make small leaves to decorate the edge, if you like, sticking them in place with a little water.) Cover and chill the dough shell for at least 1 hour.

3. Preheat the oven to 350°F.

4. Place the eggs in a large mixing bowl and beat. Beat in the honey, oatmeal, brown sugar, butter or margarine, raisins or golden raisins, pecans, cinnamon, and zest.

5. Spoon into the pie shell and smooth the surface. Bake on the middle shelf of the oven for 40–45 minutes, until a knife inserted into the middle of the filling comes out clean. Leave to cool on a wire rack for 10 minutes before serving.

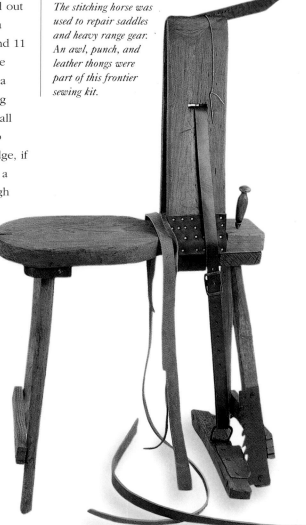

The stitching horse was used to repair saddles and heavy range gear. An awl, punch, and leather thongs were part of this frontier sewing kit.

Bread & All the Fixin's

🐂 SOURDOUGH BAKING 🐂

Folklore and romanticized legends surround the life of cowboys on the long, arduous cattle drives of the last century, but one reality that lives on in today's modern cattle industry is cowboy cooking.

Working in demanding conditions, with limited supplies and only a few ingredients, chuck wagon cooks had one of the most difficult jobs on the trail.

Cooking over open fires and using ingenious cast-iron Dutch ovens and skillets, cooks provided enough robust meals, or "chow," to feed hungry teams of up to 40 cowhands several times a day. Those simple meals eaten around a campfire under the big sky may not satisfy today's sophisticated palates, but they started a tradition

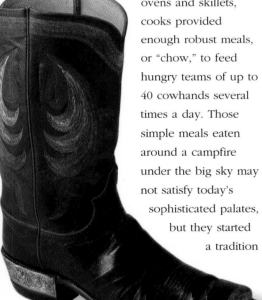

of hearty, fresh-cooked meals that continues today. One legacy of early cowboy cooking is sourdough baking.

Until yeast became commercially available in 1868, trail cooks relied on sourdough starters to make the hot bread cowpunchers expected with each meal.

Before a drive set off, each cook made a starter by combining potato cooking water and pieces of potatoes in five-gallon kegs that were set out in the hot sun each day to absorb the yeast spores naturally present in the atmosphere and set off a fermentation process. Once a starter was established, or "workin'," it became one of the cook's most precious possessions. When the weather turned cold, "biscuit-shooters," as early cooks were sometimes called, took the keg to bed with them, keeping it warm inside their bedroll.

Today, a more reliable method to establish a starter is to mix yeast with flour and water. It takes at least three days to become sour, but once established it can be kept in the refrigerator almost indefinitely, as long as it is used and replenished frequently. (See Replenishing a Sourdough Starter on the opposite page).

Sourdough Starter

Makes about 3¼ cups

1 envelope quick-rise dry yeast

½ tablespoon sugar

2 cups unbleached bread flour or all-purpose flour

2 cups water reserved from boiling potatoes, heated to 125–130°F

1. Combine the yeast, sugar, and flour in a large glass bowl. Stir in the potato water, stirring until a thick paste forms; lumps will disappear during fermentation.

2. Cover the bowl with a damp dish towel. Leave at warm room temperature for 3 days, stirring twice daily and moistening the towel, until a sour smell develops and the foam subsides. The starter will bubble and thicken, like a cake batter. Stir in any yellow skin.

3. The starter (also called a "mother starter" or "the mother") is now ready to use, and each recipe will specify the amount required. The remaining starter can be refrigerated in a covered glass container for future use.

4. When a layer of liquid develops on top of the stored starter, stir it in. If any signs of mold develops, or the starter smells rotten, discard it and start over.

Replenishing a Sourdough Starter

After the amount of starter specified in a recipe has been measured out, the leftover starter should be replenished to keep it active. This means it will not be necessary to make a new starter from scratch each time you want to bake a sourdough recipe. Replenish a starter either by stirring in fresh flour and water, or adding a portion of a sponge made in a recipe. (Sponges are made by combining the specified amount of starter with flour and water and leaving the mixture at room temperature for at least 12 hours.)

In this book, for example, the recipe for Sourdough Bread (page 69) uses the sponge technique; the recipes for Sourdough Pinch-Offs (page 68) and Sourdough Saddle Blankets (page 40) specify to replenish the reserved starter with fresh flour and water.

The reserved starter should last indefinitely if it is used and replenished regularly, ideally once every 4 days, but at least once every 2 weeks.

Using and replenishing a starter also helps it develop its "sourness," so later loaves have a more distinct flavor than the first several baked with a new starter.

Do not replenish a starter with a sponge that includes milk, eggs, butter, or any ingredients other than starter, flour, and water.

Shaping Sourdough Bread

Sourdough bread is traditionally baked as a flattened ball with a tick-tac-toe top. To shape, punch down the risen dough and turn it out onto a floured countertop. Knead the dough for about 1 minute, then shape it into a ball. Slightly flatten the ball. Rest the heel of one hand in the middle, and use your fingers to grip the top edge. Push down with the heel of your hand while your fingers pull the edge back into the middle and your other hand pushes the dough a quarter turn to the right. Continue until the ball has been pulled back on itself several times and the surface on the countertop is smooth. Turn the dough over. Follow the directions in the recipe to let the dough rise again and the directions below for scoring the top before baking.

Scoring Sourdough Bread

To make the traditional tic-tac-toe top, use a razor blade or sharp paring knife to make 2 horizontal and 2 vertical slashes about ⅛-inch deep. Make each slash with one, swift cut. Do not cut back and forth or drag the blade.

SOURDOUGH PINCH-OFFS

Makes 12 biscuits

A trail cook's reputation was often made, or lost, by the lightness of his sourdough biscuits. Early versions of these were called "pinch-offs" because cooks pinched off pieces of dough to form each biscuit, rather than roll out the dough and use cutters. This version is from Sourdough Jack's Cookery, *a 1970 collection of sourdough recipes and western folklore.*

½ cup Sourdough Starter (page 66), at room temperature

About 3 cups all-purpose flour

1 cup milk

1 tablespoon sugar

¾ teaspoon salt

1 teaspoon baking powder

½ teaspoon baking soda

1 tablespoon vegetable shortening or butter

Extra butter for the topping (optional)

1. Place the starter, 1 cup of the flour, and the milk in a glass mixing bowl and stir together. Cover with a damp dish towel and leave at room temperature for at least 8 hours. (Replenish the remaining starter with ⅓ cup of flour and 4 tablespoons of water.)

2. Melt the butter or shortening in a 3½-quart flameproof casserole 10 inches across over a medium heat. Cover to keep warm.

3. Add 1½ cups of flour, sugar, salt, baking powder, and baking soda to the sponge in the bowl. Using your hands, mix until a very soft, moist dough forms.

Add extra flour if necessary to make a dough that just holds together.

4. Turn out the dough onto a heavily floured countertop and shape into a 12-inch roll. Pinch off 12 equal pieces.

5. Working with one piece of dough at a time, and with heavily floured fingers, knead the dough into a ball. Place the ball in the pan. Continue until 12 biscuits are formed, placing each one snugly against the others and pressing down lightly so the bottom is covered; pushing the biscuits together helps to keep them soft during

baking. Lightly brush the tops with melted butter, if desired.

6. Cover and leave the biscuits to rise for about 30 minutes. Meanwhile, preheat the oven to 375°F.

7. Bake on the middle shelf of the oven, covered, for 25–30 minutes, until golden-brown and risen. Use a metal spatula to remove the biscuits from the pan. These are best served immediately.

SOURDOUGH BREAD

Makes one 3-pound loaf

Although no more difficult than conventional bread to make, sourdough bread takes longer. Be sure to allow enough time for the slow risings.

½ cup Sourdough Starter (page 66), at room temperature

About 6 cups unbleached bread flour

About ¼ cup

buttermilk

2 tablespoons butter or vegetable shortening, melted

1½ teaspoons sugar

1 teaspoon salt

1. To make a sponge, place the starter in a glass bowl and stir in 2 cups of warm (110–115°F) water. Beat in 2 cups of the flour; do not worry if any lumps remain. Cover with a damp dish towel and leave at room temperature overnight, or at least 12 hours, until it doubles in volume and is bubbly. This is the sponge.

2. Place ½ cup of the sponge in a covered container in the refrigerator for future use, or add to an existing starter (see Sourdough Baking, pages 66–67). Stir ¼ cup of buttermilk and the butter or shortening into the remaining sponge.

3. Sift 4 cups of the flour, sugar, and salt into another large mixing bowl and make a well in the middle. Pour in the sponge and, using a wooden spoon, beat together, adding extra flour or buttermilk, tablespoon by tablespoon, if necessary, until a soft dough forms.

4. Turn out the dough onto a floured countertop and knead for 10 minutes, or until smooth but soft and slightly sticky.

5. Shape into a ball and place in a greased bowl. Cover with plastic wrap and leave at room temperature, away from drafts, until it doubles in size and the indentation made by a finger remains, which can take up to 12 hours.

6. Punch down the dough. Turn it out onto a floured countertop and knead for 1 minute. Shape into a flat ball, following the directions on page 67. Place on a sheet of floured waxed paper, cover with a towel, and leave to rise until doubled in size. This can take from 1 hour to overnight, depending on the temperature and how lively the starter was.

7. Meanwhile, preheat the oven to 400°F with a baking sheet inside and a shallow roasting pan on the bottom.

8. When ready to bake, place the hot baking sheet on the stovetop. Place the dough on the waxed paper on the hot baking sheet and sprinkle with flour. Score a tic-tac-toe pattern on top, following the directions on page 67.

9. Pour 2 cups of water into the roasting pan. Bake on a low shelf for 20 minutes. Lower the temperature to 350°F and continue baking for 35–40 minutes, until the loaf is well risen, golden brown, and sounds hollow when tapped on the bottom. Leave to cool on a wire rack.

CHUNKY SKILLET CORNBREAD
Makes 6–8 servings

*Any trail team with a Mexican or southern cook would have eaten cornbread served straight
from a Dutch oven along with the ubiquitous sourdough bread and biscuits.*

4 tablespoons vegetable oil or rendered bacon fat

1 cup yellow cornmeal

1 cup all-purpose flour

1½ tablespoons sugar

1 tablespoon baking powder

½ teaspoon salt

½ cup finely sliced green part of green onions (scallions)

½ cup fresh corn kernels or well-drained canned kernels

1 cup buttermilk

1 egg, lightly beaten

1. Preheat the oven to 425°F. Heat the oil or bacon fat in a 9-inch skillet with an ovenproof handle over medium heat. Swirl the pan to coat the bottom and side.

2. Place the cornmeal, flour, sugar, baking powder, and salt in a bowl and stir together. Stir in the green onions (scallions) and corn kernels.

3. Make a well in the middle and pour in the buttermilk, egg, and remaining hot oil or fat from the skillet. Stir together until just combined. Spoon into the hot skillet and smooth the surface.

4. Bake in the oven on the middle shelf for about 25 minutes, or until a wooden toothpick stuck into the middle comes out clean. Serve straight from the skillet, or turn out onto a wire rack and leave to cool to room temperature.

Variation

To vary the cornbread, replace the buttermilk with 1 cup of sour cream. Alternatively, for a more contemporary-style bread, stir in 3 finely chopped, well-drained sun-dried tomatoes packed in oil.

COOK'S TIPS

To serve the cornbread as part of a barbecue, make in advance and leave to cool. About 20 minutes before you are ready to serve, wrap the cornbread in foil and reheat on the grill rack.

If you are out of buttermilk, add 1 tablespoon of lemon juice to enough milk to make 1 cup in a measuring jug, and let stand for about 5 minutes.

The cowboy's harness consisted of a leather headstall and a curb bit. The headstall was slipped over the ears, and because the bit was often sharp, the horse could be guided by a flick of the reins. Heavy leather work gloves completed the cowboy uniform.

MONTEREY JACK SODA BREAD

Makes 4 servings

*The many Irish men looking for adventure in the Wild West who ended up cooking on ranches
introduced this quick-and-easy bread.
Monterey Jack is a mild cheese. For a fuller flavor, substitute a sharp cheddar cheese, or use
Colby cheese, which will leave pale orange specks through the crumb.*

1½ cups whole-wheat flour

1½ cups unbleached bread flour

1 tablespoon sugar

1 teaspoon baking soda

1 teaspoon baking powder

½ teaspoon salt

3 tablespoons chilled butter, diced

½ cup finely shredded Monterey Jack cheese

1¼–1½ cups buttermilk

4 tablespoons freshly snipped chives

1. Preheat the oven to 375°F. Sift the flours, sugar, baking soda, baking powder, and salt into a large mixing bowl, tipping in any bran left behind in the sieve. Cut in the butter until coarse crumbs form. Stir in ¼ cup of the cheese.

2. Stir in 1¼ cups of the buttermilk and mix to form a thick dough. Add a little extra buttermilk if necessary, tablespoon by tablespoon. Turn out the dough onto a lightly floured countertop and knead until it just forms a smooth ball, kneading in the chives. Do not overknead at this point or the bread will be heavy.

3. Place the dough on a heavily floured baking sheet and press down to flatten slightly. Sprinkle with the remaining cheese. Using a floured knife, cut an "X" in the top of the dough, without cutting all the way through it.

4. Bake on the middle shelf of the oven for 35–40 minutes, until well risen, golden brown, and sounds hollow when tapped on the bottom. Leave to cool slightly on a wire rack. Serve warm or at room temperature, broken into 4 pieces.

72

BACON 'N' CHEESE BEER LOAF

Makes 1 large loaf

Daily bread baking continues as a regular part of many ranch cooks' days. This quick batter bread can be fitted into the busiest schedule, and makes a light loaf that is delicious when toasted. Sprinkling the pan with cornmeal prevents the cheese melting onto the sides of the pan, which would make it difficult to turn out the loaf.

Butter, for greasing the pan

Yellow cornmeal

6 slices cured or smoked bacon

3 cups all-purpose flour

2½ teaspoons baking powder

2 tablespoons sugar

1 cup shredded sharp cheddar, Monterey Jack, or Colby cheese

One 12-ounce bottle beer

Butter for serving (optional)

1. Heat the oven to 350°F. Grease a 9 x 5 x 2-inch bread pan and sprinkle yellow cornmeal over the bottom and sides. Tap out any excess.

2. Put the bacon slices in a large skillet over medium-high heat. Fry, turning once, for 6 minutes, or until the bacon is cooked through but not crisp. Remove from the pan and drain well on paper towels. Finely dice the bacon. Set aside.

3. Sift the flour, baking powder, and sugar into a large mixing bowl. Stir in ¾ cup of the cheese. Make a well in the middle and stir in the beer to form a stiff batter. Stir in the bacon but do not beat.

4. Spoon the batter into the prepared pan, dropping it in mounds so the loaf has a rugged-looking top. Bake on the middle shelf of the oven for 30 minutes. Sprinkle the top with the remaining cheese and continue baking for 10 minutes, until well risen, golden brown, and sounds hollow when tapped on the bottom. Leave to cool in the pan for 5 minutes. Turn out and leave to cool slightly on a wire rack. Serve warm or at room temperature, with butter if desired.

73

MAPLE-PECAN BREAKFAST ROLLS

Makes 12 rolls

Breakfasts on ranches have always been hearty affairs, served as early as three o'clock in the morning in the early days of ranching. These satisfyingly sweet rolls can be shaped and refrigerated overnight for early morning baking. Leave them for one hour at warm room temperature before you bake them.

1 cup milk

¼ cup butter

About 2½ cups all-purpose flour

1 tablespoon sugar

1 teaspoon salt

1 envelope quick-rise dry yeast

1 large egg, lightly beaten

2 tablespoons maple syrup, melted, plus extra for brushing

1 cup chopped pecans

¾ cup golden raisins

2 tablespoons finely grated orange zest

2 teaspoons apple pie spice

1. Place the milk in a small saucepan over medium heat and heat to 125–130°F. Add the butter to the pan and stir until completely melted.

2. Sift the flour, sugar, and salt into a large mixing bowl. Stir in the yeast and make a well in the middle. Pour in the melted butter, milk, and egg. Using a wooden spoon, beat together, adding extra flour, tablespoon by tablespoon, if necessary, until a soft dough forms. Adding too much flour will result in heavy rolls.

3. Turn out the dough onto a lightly floured countertop and knead for 10 minutes, until smooth but still soft.

4. Shape the dough into a ball and place in a lightly greased bowl. Cover with plastic wrap and leave at room temperature, away from drafts, until the dough doubles in size and the indentation made by a finger remains. Meanwhile, grease a 9 x 11-inch baking pan.

5. Punch down the dough. Turn it out onto a lightly floured countertop and knead for 1 minute. Roll out into a 12-inch square.

6. Brush the dough with the maple syrup, leaving a ¼-inch border all around. Scatter with the pecans, golden raisins, orange zest, and apple pie spice. Roll up like a jelly roll.

7. Using a floured, sharp knife, cut the roll into 12 equal slices.

Place the slices, cut edge up, in the pan, snugly against each other. Press down lightly. Cover with plastic wrap and leave to rise until doubled in size.

8. Meanwhile, heat the oven to 400°F. Bake on the middle shelf for 25 minutes, or until well risen and golden brown. Turn out and transfer to a wire rack. Brush the top with a thin layer of maple syrup and leave to cool slightly. Separate the rolls and serve warm or at room temperature.

TEX-MEX CRANBERRY SALSA

Makes about 1¼ cups

The sharp flavor of cranberries with the sweetness of fresh orange juice and the heat of chiles makes this ideal to serve with full-flavored game, such as venison, buffalo, or moose, or wild turkey steaks. This can be made up to a day in advance, but be sure to store it in a glass jar or bowl without a metal lid.

2 cups cranberries, thawed if frozen

1 Anaheim or green chile, unseeded and chopped

Finely pared strips of zest from 1 large orange, without any white pith

3 tablespoons sugar

2 tablespoons distilled white vinegar

1½–2 tablespoons freshly squeezed orange juice

Salt, to taste

Finely snipped fresh chives, to garnish

1. Place the cranberries, chile, orange zest, and sugar in a food processor and pulse until finely chopped.

2. Transfer to a glass bowl. Using a wooden spoon, stir in the vinegar, 1½ tablespoons of orange juice, and salt. Taste and add more orange juice if necessary. Leave to stand for at least 20 minutes before serving, sprinkled with the snipped chives.

SORREL SAUCE

Makes about ½ cup

Fresh sorrel is a natural partner for Planked Salmon (page 50) or any grilled or baked salmon. This quickly prepared sauce also goes well with simply cooked tuna or cod steaks.

½ cup butter

1 large handful fresh sorrel leaves, stems removed and leaves finely shredded

½ fresh lemon

Salt and freshly ground black pepper, to taste

1. Melt the butter in a small saucepan over medium heat or on the side of the barbecue rack, stirring if necessary. Add the sorrel and cook, stirring, for about 1 minute, until just starting to wilt.

2. Squeeze in lemon juice to taste, then add salt and pepper. Remove from the heat and serve at once.

76

CHILE BREAD-AND-BUTTER PICKLES

Makes enough to fill four 1½-cup jars

3 cups sugar

1 cup distilled white vinegar

10 dried red chiles

10 cloves garlic, halved, green cores removed, and thinly sliced

10 cloves

4 fresh bay leaves

2 teaspoons black mustard seeds, crushed

2 teaspoons coriander seeds, lightly crushed

1 teaspoon black peppercorns, lightly crushed

3¾ pounds pickling cucumbers in brine, well drained and cut into ¼-inch slices

1. Place the sugar in a large glass bowl. Using a wooden spoon, stir in the vinegar. Continue stirring until the sugar dissolves and the mixture no longer appears sludgy.

2. Add the chiles, garlic, cloves, bay leaves, mustard seeds, coriander seeds, peppercorns, and cucumber slices.

3. Cover the bowl with plastic wrap and leave in a cool, dark place for at least one week. Transfer to 1½-cup jars, seal, and store for up to 2 months.

PICKLED MIXED VEGETABLES

Makes enough to fill two 1-quart jars

2 quarts cider vinegar

2½ cups sugar

1½ tablespoons mustard seeds

½ tablespoon coriander seeds

½ tablespoon black peppercorns

6 cloves

4 dried red chiles

2 dried bay leaves, torn in half

3 cups small cauliflower flowerets

2 cups chopped green beans

4 carrots, peeled and sliced

2 red, yellow, or orange bell peppers, cored, seeded, and chopped

1. Place the vinegar and sugar in a large saucepan over medium-high heat. Stir in 1½ quarts of water and bring to a boil, stirring until the sugar dissolves. Lower the heat, stir in the mustard seeds, coriander seeds, peppercorns, cloves, chiles, and bay leaves, and simmer, uncovered, for 30 minutes.

2. Meanwhile, sterilize two 1-quart preserving jars by boiling them in a large saucepan or flameproof casserole in water to cover for 10 minutes. Leave in the water until ready to fill.

3. Wearing oven mitts and using tongs, lift the jars from the hot water and pour away the water. Spoon a mixture of cauliflower flowerets, green beans, carrots, bell peppers, and the flavoring ingredients into the hot jars to within ½ inch of the top. Ladle the simmering liquid over the vegetables to ¼ inch from the top. Tap the jars on the countertop to remove any air bubbles.

4. Seal the jars following the manufacturer's directions. Store in a cool place for at least 1 week before serving. These will keep for up to 3 months.

BROOKVILLE COLESLAW

Makes 4–6 servings

4 cups very thinly sliced green cabbage

¼ cup sugar

3 tablespoons cider or white-wine vinegar

¼ teaspoon salt

Freshly ground black pepper, to taste

½ cup heavy cream, whipped until soft peaks form

Finely chopped fresh parsley or coriander (cilantro), to garnish

1. Place the cabbage, sugar, vinegar, salt, and pepper in a large bowl and toss together. Cover with plastic wrap and refrigerate for at least 1 hour.

2. Fold in the whipped cream. Taste and adjust the sugar, vinegar, or salt as necessary. Transfer to a serving bowl. Sprinkle with parsley or coriander (cilantro).

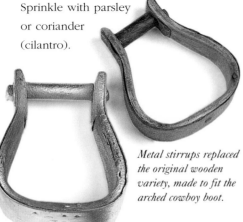

Metal stirrups replaced the original wooden variety, made to fit the arched cowboy boot.

CAMPFIRE BBQ SAUCE

Makes about 2 cups

1 cup bottled tomato sauce

¾ cup cider vinegar

1 onion, very finely chopped

2 cloves garlic, halved, green cores removed, and crushed

4 tablespoons Worcestershire sauce

1 tablespoon light brown sugar

1 teaspoon salt

¾ teaspoon dry mustard

½ teaspoon cayenne pepper, or to taste

Freshly ground black pepper, to taste

2 tablespoons butter or vegetable oil

1. Place the tomato sauce, vinegar, onion, garlic, Worcestershire sauce, sugar, salt, mustard, cayenne pepper, and black pepper in a pan over medium-high heat. Stir in ½ cup of water and bring to a boil, stirring with a wooden spoon, until all the ingredients are well blended.

2. Lower the heat, partially cover the pan, and simmer for about 15 minutes, stirring occasionally.

3. Remove from the heat and stir in the butter or oil. Use the sauce at once, or leave to cool and refrigerate until required. Reheat to use.

SOUTH-OF-THE-BORDER SALSA

Makes about 3 cups

6 large tomatoes, unseeded and diced

4 green onions (scallions), quartered lengthwise and finely sliced

1 large clove garlic, halved, green core removed, and very finely chopped

½–1 bird's-eye red chile, unseeded and finely chopped

1 tablespoon finely grated lime zest

1 tablespoon lime juice

½ teaspoon ground cumin

Chopped fresh coriander (cilantro), to serve

1. Place all the ingredients in a glass bowl and stir together with a wooden spoon. Leave to stand at room temperature for at least 20 minutes.

2. Transfer to a nonmetallic serving dish. Sprinkle with coriander (cilantro).

CORN-ZUCCHINI SALAD

Makes 4–6 servings

3 tablespoons vegetable oil

2 tablespoons cider vinegar

1 tablespoon prepared mustard

Salt and freshly ground black pepper, to taste

Freshly cut kernels from 6 ears of corn, about 3 cups, or 1½ (11-ounce) cans corn kernels, drained

3 zucchini, cut into ¼-inch dice

1 cup diced radishes

2 green onions (scallions), finely sliced

4 tablespoons finely shredded fresh basil

1. Place the vegetable oil, vinegar, mustard, and salt and pepper in a salad bowl and beat until well blended.

2. Meanwhile, bring a saucepan of water to a boil over high heat. Add the corn and boil for 2 minutes. Add the zucchini and boil for 1 minute longer, or until both vegetables are just tender-crisp. Drain well.

3. Immediately add the hot vegetables to the salad bowl and stir until well coated in the dressing. Set aside to cool.

4. Stir in the radishes, green onions (scallions), and basil. Serve the salad at once.

Index

Acknowledgments

Footnotes
On the Trail
1: Adams, Ramon F., Come an' Get It, The Story of the Old Cowboy Cook, page 88.
2: Adams, Andy, The Log of a Cowboy, page 311.
3: Adams, Ramon F., Come an' Get It, page 101

At the Ranch and Trailhead
1: Brown Dee, The American West, page 297.
2: Adams, Ramon F., Come an' Get It, page 117.

Author's acknowledgments
First and foremost I must thank my husband, Philip Beck, who shopped and tested; Tim Back, who tested all the barbecue recipes; and Henry Johnson, who tested bread recipes. Thanks also go to David Healy, of Washington, D.C., for advice and his family's coleslaw recipe; Cathy Luchetti, Jo Richardson; and Carl Cullingford, Philip Dudden, Maggi Gordon, and Stefanie Roth, for providing recipes, difficult-to-locate ingredients, and/or ideas; and Liz Wolf-Cohen and Amanda Heywood, for making the food look so great.

Publisher's ackowledgments
The Publishers wish to thank the following collectors and picture libraries who have supplied the photographs (and/or items for photography) that are featured in the book.
Mr. Yeargin, Star Saddlery: pages 6, 9, 12, 14, 16, 18, 20, 22, 24, 28, 30, 33, 39, 40, 42, 45, 46, 49, 50, 52, 55, 56, 58, 61, 62, 67, 70, 72, 73, 74, 76, 78.
Peter Newark's Western Americana: endpapers, pages 2, 7, 8, 10–11, 37–38.
Kansas State Historical Society: pages 65-66.
The Stock Broker: page 66.